D095580b

Written by Genny Monchamp

Illustrated by Karol Kaminski

SHINE

Choices to Make God Smile

Pauline
BOOKS & MEDIA
Boston

Library of Congress Cataloging-in-Publication Data

Monchamp, Genny.
Shine : choices to make God smile / written by Genny Monchamp ; illustrated
by Karol Kaminski.
p. cm.
ISBN 0-8198-7149-4
1. Conduct of life—Juvenile literature. 2. Children—Religious life—Juvenile
literature. I. Kaminski, Karol. II. Title.
BJ1581.2.M585 2011
248.8′2—dc22
      2011011136

The Scripture quotations contained herein are from the *New Revised Standard
Version Bible: Catholic Edition,* copyright © 1989, 1993, Division of Chris-
tian Education of the National Council of the Churches of Christ in the United
States of America. Used by permission. All rights reserved.

Illustrated by Karol Kaminski
Design by Mary Joseph Peterson, FSP

Published by Pauline Books & Media, 50 Saint Pauls Avenue, Boston, MA
02130-3491

Printed in the U.S.A.

SCGS VSAUSAPEOILL5-2610045 7149-4

www.pauline.org

Pauline Books & Media is the publishing house of the Daughters of St. Paul,
an international congregation of women religious serving the Church with the
communications media.

2 3 4 5 6 7 8 9   19 18 17 16 15

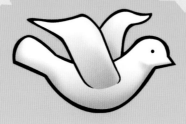

The fruit of the
Holy Spirit is love,
joy, peace, patience,
kindness, goodness,
faithfulness, gentleness,
and self-control.

cf. Galatians 5:22–23

Every morning
God puts the sun in
the sky to shine.

God put a light
in me too.

When I show his love to the world,
I SHINE!

My sister needs help with her chores.

Should I help her even if I don't like to dust?

YES!

God wants me to love others and do nice things.

When I love others, God smiles and **I SHINE!**

Josie won the race again.

Should I be grumpy because I didn't win?

NO!

God wants me to have joy even when I don't win.

When I show joy to others, God smiles and **I SHINE!**

Kitty didn't come in tonight.

Should I go to sleep even though I'm worried?

YES!

God wants me to have peace because he is in control.

I say a prayer for kitty before I go to sleep.

When I have peace, God smiles and **I SHINE!**

I want to tell my teacher something, but she's talking.

Should I interrupt her?

God wants me to be patient and respect my teacher.

I wait until she is done talking and then tell her my news.

When I am patient, God smiles and **I SHINE!**

My dog's food dish is empty.

Should I feed Oliver before I go out to play?

YES!

God wants me to be kind
to people and animals.

I feed Oliver and
then go out to play.

When I am kind,
God smiles and
I SHINE!

Mom wants to give away my old toys.

Should I share them with kids who don't have any toys?

YES!

God wants me to be good to others, even if I don't know them.

When I am good to others, God smiles and **I SHINE!**

I told Will that I would play
with him at recess.

Now I want to play with
Erin instead.

Should I play with Erin instead of Will?

NO!

God wants me to be faithful and keep my promises.

I play with Will and Erin at recess.

When I am faithful, God smiles and **I SHINE!**

My brother lost my favorite ball.

I am so mad that I want to yell at him.
Should I?

God wants me to be gentle with my words.

I ask my brother to please help me look for the ball.

When I am gentle, God smiles and **I SHINE!**

Dad baked my favorite cookies.

Can I sneak just one before dinner?

NO! God wants me to have self-control.

I eat all my dinner and then ask for a cookie.

When I have self-control, God smiles and **I SHINE!**

God loves me all the time, even when I make mistakes.

But I really love to make him smile.

It makes him happy to make me **SHINE!**

For Kids

In this book, you have learned about the fruit of the Spirit: love, joy, peace, patience, kindness, goodness, faithfulness, gentleness, and self-control. When we see someone choose to act in those ways, we are seeing God's Holy Spirit alive and at work in that person's life.

You make choices every day. Because God loves you and wants what's best for you, he has sent his Holy Spirit to help you make choices that are right and wise—choices that will make your heart "fruitful."

Do you know that happy feeling in your heart when you do something good? That's the Holy Spirit telling you that you're making good choices. When you think about doing something wrong and you get that funny feeling in your tummy, that's the Holy Spirit too, helping you to make a better choice.

The Holy Spirit reminds you to make good choices. He also gives you the grace and power to be the kind of person God made you to be.

Sometimes, we're not sure what choices to make. Whenever you don't know what to do, stop, pray, and ask God to help. Choose what kind of person you want to be. Remember that God loves you all of the time and he wants you to **SHINE!**

—Genny

For Grown-Ups

Adults are the first and most influential teachers of the children in their lives. But in our world, "train[ing] children in the right way" (Proverbs 22:6) is as challenging as ever. How can we show children how to make decisions that are not only morally right, but also godly and wise? How do we teach our children to "shine like the brightness of the sky" (Daniel 12:3)?

Shine can help to engage both adults and children in the formation of strong Christian character. Each of the realistic scenarios presented in *Shine* is framed in an interactive question format. When children independently answer questions related to moral and character formation, they build the self-respect and confidence necessary for them to make wise decisions in the real world. Through the choices they make in *Shine*, children become equipped to live in a way that glorifies God and makes them "shine." They begin to understand that the choices they make define the kind of person they are becoming.

Shine encourages children to draw on the "fruit of the Spirit" (Galatians 5:22–23) in their daily lives. My hope is that this book will help children recognize real situations that call them to respond with: love, joy, peace, patience, kindness, goodness, faithfulness, gentleness, and self-control. The fundamental lessons children learn about a fruitful spirit in *Shine* will apply to their lives forever. Even as a child outgrows the scenarios in the book, the lessons learned about the graces of the Holy Spirit endure. Be encouraged that this same Spirit is with you as you guide the children he has entrusted to your care.

—*Genny Monchamp*

Who are the Daughters of St. Paul?

We are Catholic sisters. Our mission is to be like Saint Paul and tell everyone about Jesus! There are so many ways for people to communicate with each other. We want to use all of them so everyone will know how much God loves us. We do this by printing books (you're holding one!), making radio shows, singing, helping people at our bookstores, using the Internet, and in many other ways.

Visit our Web site at www.pauline.org

Genevieve Monchamp lives, writes, and plays in sunny northern California with her husband, Clint, three daughters, Kylie, Madison, and Avery, and her tortoise, Lettuce Lips. She is the author of *God Made Wonderful Me* (Pauline Books & Media, 2008)and is currently working on her next inspirational children's book.

"Arise, shine, for your light has come, and the glory of the LORD rises upon you."
Isaiah 60:1

Diana Vader Photography

Karol Kaminski has been drawing and creating characters ever since she was a young girl. After earning her BFA in drawing and painting from Baldwin–Wallace College, she worked as a sign painter, cartoonist, graphic designer, and an art director for an advertising agency.

For the past twenty years, Karol's work has appeared in books and magazines, on posters, wallpaper, puzzles, games, stickers, and greeting cards, as well as in advertising campaigns. No stranger to Pauline Books & Media, Karol is the illustrator of *God Made Wonderful Me* (2008).

When she isn't drawing or painting, Karol is a teacher and coach, and she spends her free time reading books to children at the school library and teaching little ones how to draw.

Karol lives with her husband, Stacy, her children Alyssa, Alex, Kyra, and Eli and their pooch, Angus, in Brunswick, Ohio—just south of Cleveland!

ILLUSTRATED BY

Pauline
BOOKS & MEDIA

The Daughters of St. Paul operate book and media centers at the following addresses. Visit, call, or write the one nearest you today, or find us at www.pauline.org

CALIFORNIA
3908 Sepulveda Blvd, Culver City, CA 90230 — 310-397-8676
935 Brewster Avenue, Redwood City, CA 94063 — 650-369-4230
5945 Balboa Avenue, San Diego, CA 92111 — 858-565-9181

FLORIDA
145 S.W. 107th Avenue, Miami, FL 33174 — 305-559-6715

HAWAII
1143 Bishop Street, Honolulu, HI 96813 — 808-521-2731

ILLINOIS
172 North Michigan Avenue, Chicago, IL 60601 — 312-346-4228

LOUISIANA
4403 Veterans Memorial Blvd, Metairie, LA 70006 — 504-887-7631

MASSACHUSETTS
885 Providence Hwy, Dedham, MA 02026 — 781-326-5385

MISSOURI
9804 Watson Road, St. Louis, MO 63126 — 314-965-3512

NEW YORK
64 W. 38th Street, New York, NY 10018 — 212-754-1110

SOUTH CAROLINA
243 King Street, Charleston, SC 29401 — 843-577-0175

TEXAS
Currently no book center; for parish exhibits or outreach evangelization, contact: 210-569-0500, or SanAntonio@paulinemedia.com, or P.O. Box 761416, San Antonio, TX 78245

VIRGINIA
1025 King Street, Alexandria, VA 22314 — 703-549-3806

CANADA
3022 Dufferin Street, Toronto, ON M6B 3T5 — 416-781-9131

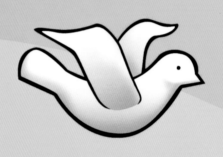